My Very Own
VALENTINE'S DAY

A Book of
Cooking and Crafts

My Very Own

HOLIDAY
BOOKS

My Very Own

VALENTINE'S DAY

A Book of
Cooking and Crafts

by Robin West

photographs by Robert L. and Diane Wolfe
illustrations by Susan Slattery Burke

Carolrhoda Books, Inc./Minneapolis

To Marbles Northstar

Library of Congress Cataloging-in-Publication Data

West, Robin.
    My very own Valentine's Day: a book of cooking and
crafts / by Robin West ; photographs by Robert L. and
Diane Wolfe ; illustrations by Susan Slattery Burke.
        p.   cm. — (My very own holiday books)
    Includes index.
    Summary: Includes recipes and craft ideas for
Valentine's Day and information about the holiday.
    ISBN 0-87614-724-4
    1. Holiday cookery—Juvenile literature. 2. Menus—
Juvenile literature. 3. Valentine decorations—Juvenile
literature. [1. Valentine's Day. 2. Cookery.
3. Valentine's decorations.] I. Wolfe, Robert L., ill.
II. Wolfe, Diane, ill. III. Burke, Susan Slattery, ill.
IV. Title. V. Series.
TX739.W47 1992
641.5'68—dc20   92-22254
                                                      CIP
                                                       AC

Manufactured in the United States of America

1   2   3   4   5   6   98   97   96   95   94   93

Contents

Valentine Greetings

Hearts and flowers, candles and lace . . . Valentine's Day can be so romantic. Too mushy for you? Add balloons and confetti and boxes of chocolate, and Valentine's Day can be lots of fun!

You don't have to wait for February 14 for the Valentine fun to begin. Getting ready for Valentine's Day can be almost as much fun as the holiday itself. Make a festive centerpiece for your table or a valentine for a special friend. You might even try having a party and making the food yourself (with a little help from an adult friend). The ideas are endless so you'd better get started, because Valentine's Day will be here before you know it!

Make It Your Very Own:
How to Use this Book

RECIPES

The recipes in this book are divided into five menus, but you don't have to make a whole meal.
If you are a new cook, start slowly. Choose a recipe that sounds good to you and try it out. You might need lots of help to begin with, but be patient. The more you practice, the better you'll be.

Here are some of the easier recipes to get you started:

Strawberry Surprise Punch
Crazy Crackers
Not Just a Peanut Butter Sandwich
Coconut Dreams

Once you know what you're doing, it's time to make a whole meal. Try one of the menus, or put together your own combination.

Here are some things to consider when planning a menu:

Nutrition: Balance your menu by choosing something from each of the four food groups: breads, dairy products, fruits and vegetables, and meat and other proteins. You can fill out your menu with foods that don't need recipes, such as bread, fresh fruit, milk, cheese, and raw vegetables.

Variety: Include different tastes and textures in your meal. If one food is soft and creamy, serve it with something crunchy. Salty foods taste good when served with something sweet. Try to include a variety of colors so the food is as pretty to look at as it is good to eat.

Theme: Each of the menus in this

book has a theme, just to make it more fun. Try to think up a theme of your own, and choose recipes that go with it. How about a menu of foods that can be eaten with your fingers? Why not serve a meal made up of different kinds of fruit? (Be sure to put Valentine Fruit Pizza on your list.) Or forget about planning a meal, and make a variety of desserts instead. Anything is possible!

Be sure to share your masterpiece with someone else. Whether you make one dish or an entire meal, half the fun of cooking is watching someone else enjoy the food.

CRAFTS

Like the recipes, all of the crafts in this book are easy to make, but some are easier than others. If you haven't tried making crafts before, start with something easy, like a Hearts and Flowers Bouquet or a Three-D Valentine. As you gain confidence, put together a Mousy Valentine or a Heartful Mobile. Once you've tackled these crafts, you're ready for the Candyman.

Don't be afraid to use your imagination when decorating your crafts. Use markers, colored construction paper, scraps of fabric, or even glitter to give your craft a personal touch.

Cooking Smart

Valentine's Day is a time for surprises, but you don't want them to happen while you're cooking. Whether you are a new or experienced cook, these cooking tips can help you avoid a kitchen disaster.

BEFORE YOU COOK

- Get yourself ready. If you have long hair, tie it back to keep it out of the food, away from flames, and out of your way. Roll up your sleeves, and put on an apron. And be sure to wash your hands well with soap.
- Read through the entire recipe and assemble all of the ingredients. It's no fun to find out halfway through a recipe that you're out of eggs.
- Go through the recipe with an adult helper and decide which steps you can perform yourself and which you'll need help with.

WHILE YOU COOK

- Raw meat and raw eggs can contain dangerous bacteria. Wash your hands and any utensils or cutting boards you've used after handling these raw foods. Never put cooked meat on an unwashed plate that has held raw meat. Any dough that contains raw eggs isn't safe to eat until it's cooked.
- Keep cold foods in the refrigerator until you need them.
- Wash fruits and vegetables thoroughly before using them.
- Turn pot handles to the back of the stove so the pots won't be knocked off by accident. When you are taking the lid off a hot pan, always keep the opening away from your face so the steam won't burn you.
- Use a potholder when handling hot pans. Be sure the potholder is

dry before you use it. The heat from the pan will come right through a wet potholder.

- Always turn off the stove or oven as soon as you're done with it.
- Be careful with foods when they come out of the microwave. Although the food may seem to be cool to the touch, microwaving can produce hot spots. When you're heating a liquid in the microwave, stir it often to distribute the heat evenly.
- Only use microwave-safe dishes in the microwave. Never put anything metal in the microwave.
- Don't cut up food in your hand. Use a cutting board.
- Carry knives point down.
- Be careful when opening cans. The edges of the lids are very sharp.
- Don't save the mess for the end. Try to clean up as you go along.

AFTER YOU COOK

- Once you've finished cooking, be sure to store your creation in the refrigerator if it contains any ingredients that might spoil.
- Be a courteous cook: clean up your mess. Leave the kitchen looking as clean as (or cleaner than) you found it.

SOME CRAFTY TIPS

Assembling a craft is a lot like cooking, and many of the same tips apply. Read the instructions and gather your supplies before you start. Play it safe with your supplies, especially scissors, and be sure to get an adult friend to help you when you need it. Put down newspapers to protect your work surface. And, of course, be sure to clean up your mess when you're done.

Be My Old-Fashioned Valentine

Pork Chops Parmesan

Perfect Potato Casserole

Very-Berry Freeze Pie

Hearts and Flowers Bouquet

Pork Chops Parmesan

YOU WILL NEED:

¹/₄ cup butter

1 cup bread crumbs

3 tablespoons Parmesan cheese

¹/₂ teaspoon salt

¹/₈ teaspoon pepper

4 tablespoons milk

2 eggs, beaten

6 pork chops

1 Preheat oven to 325°.

2 Place butter in a 9- by 13-inch baking pan and melt butter in oven while preheating.

3 In a shallow bowl, combine bread crumbs, Parmesan cheese, salt, and pepper. Stir well.

4 In a second shallow bowl, combine milk and eggs and stir well.

5 Coat each pork chop first with crumb mixture, then with eggs, then with crumbs again.

6 Arrange pork chops in baking pan on top of melted butter. Pork chops shouldn't touch.

7 Bake for 30 minutes on one side. Turn pork chops over and bake for another 30 minutes or until pork chops are tender.

Serves 6

Perfect Potato Casserole

YOU WILL NEED:

4 large potatoes, peeled and thinly sliced

1/4 cup butter

1 cup milk

1 tablespoon Worcestershire sauce

2 tablespoons flour

1 cup shredded cheddar cheese

1 Preheat oven to 350°.

2 Arrange potato slices in a medium casserole dish.

3 In a small saucepan, melt butter over medium-low heat. Add milk and Worcestershire sauce and stir.

4 Stir in flour little by little. Cook for about 5 minutes, stirring constantly, until mixture begins to thicken.

5 Pour milk mixture over the potatoes and cover.

6 Bake for 1 hour.

7 Sprinkle with cheese and bake uncovered for 5 minutes or until cheese has melted.

Serves 4 to 6

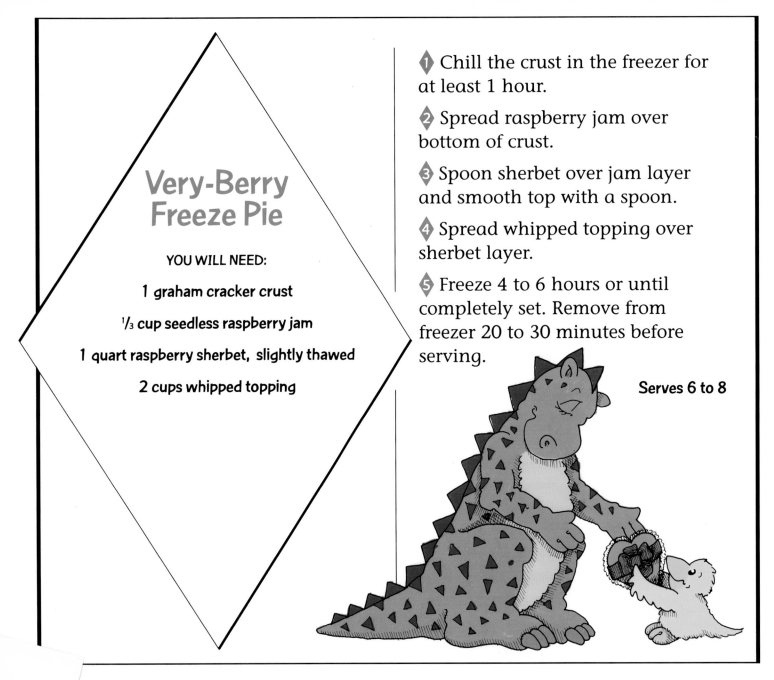

Very-Berry Freeze Pie

YOU WILL NEED:

1 graham cracker crust

$\frac{1}{3}$ cup seedless raspberry jam

1 quart raspberry sherbet, slightly thawed

2 cups whipped topping

1 Chill the crust in the freezer for at least 1 hour.

2 Spread raspberry jam over bottom of crust.

3 Spoon sherbet over jam layer and smooth top with a spoon.

4 Spread whipped topping over sherbet layer.

5 Freeze 4 to 6 hours or until completely set. Remove from freezer 20 to 30 minutes before serving.

Serves 6 to 8

Hearts and Flowers Bouquet

YOU WILL NEED:

tracing paper

pencil

scissors

construction paper (red, pink, and white)

ruler

white liquid glue

decorating materials such as lace, ribbons, sequins, and glitter

clear-drying glue (look for Super Tacky glue in sewing and craft stores)

3 4-inch green pipe cleaners

masking tape (optional)

1 small magnet

THE VASE:

1 Place tracing paper on top of figure A on page 19 and trace. Cut out tracing paper pattern.

2 Place the pattern on red construction paper and trace around it. Cut out construction paper figure. This figure will be used to make a heart-shaped vase.

3 Mark construction paper figure with dots pictured on figure A. Use a ruler to draw a line connecting dot 1 and dot 2. Then connect dot 2 and dot 3.

4 Fold on these lines to make flap Y and flap Z, keeping the lines on the insides of the folds.

⑤ Glue flap Y to flap Z with white liquid glue as shown.

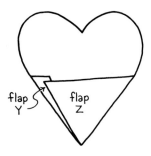

⑥ Decorate the heart using such materials as lace and ribbons, attached with clear-drying glue.

THE FLOWERS:

① Place tracing paper on top of figure B on page 19 and trace. Cut out tracing paper pattern.

② Place the pattern on red, pink, or white construction paper and trace around it. Move pattern and trace around it again. Repeat one more time to make a third heart.

③ Cut out construction paper hearts. These will be used to make heart-shaped "flowers."

④ Decorate flowers using such materials as lace and ribbons, attached with clear-drying glue.

⑤ Using clear-drying glue, glue one end of a pipe cleaner to the back of each heart-shaped flower to make a stem. Hold in place until glue sets.

TO ASSEMBLE:

① Use clear-drying glue to attach pipe cleaner stems to the back of the vase as shown. You may want to make the stems extra secure with masking tape once the glue has set.

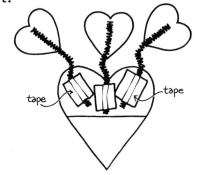

❷ Using clear-drying glue, attach the magnet to the back of the vase as shown. Hold in place until the glue sets.

❸ Bend the pipe cleaners in an interesting way to give the flowers life.

There's plenty of room in your valentine vase for candy, dried flowers, or even a secret note.

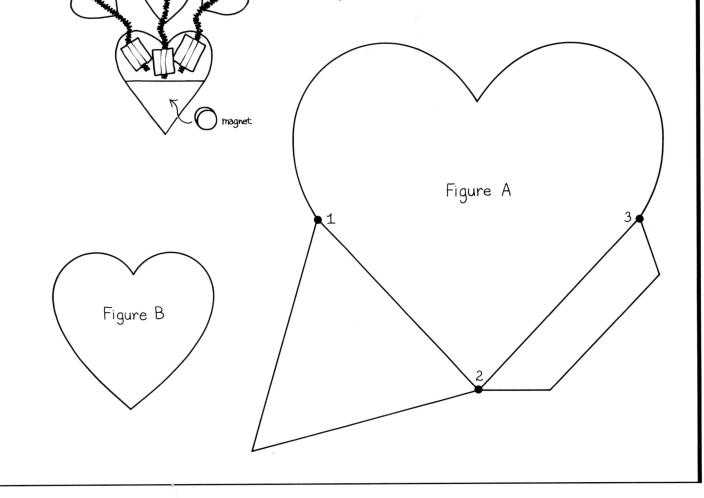

magnet

Figure A

Figure B

1

2

3

A Wild and Wacky Valentine

Dizzy Ham Wheels

▼

Crazy Crackers

▼

Strawberry Surprise Punch

▼

Nutty Banana Pops

▼

The Candyman

Dizzy Ham Wheels

YOU WILL NEED:

1 can refrigerator crescent rolls
(8 rolls per package)

4 slices boiled ham

8 slices American or cheddar cheese

milk

sesame seeds or poppy seeds

SPECIAL EQUIPMENT:

toothpicks

❶ Preheat oven to temperature called for on crescent roll package.

❷ Separate rolls into four squares. Press the perforated diagonal lines together with your thumbs so the squares are solid. Place squares on ungreased baking sheet.

❸ Cut ham and cheese into 1½-inch squares. Top each square of dough with a slice of cheese, then a slice of ham, then another slice of cheese.

❹ With each square of dough, make a cut from each of the four corners toward the center. Stop ½ inch from the center.

❺ With each square of dough, fold alternating points to center as shown. Overlap each point of dough over the last one and pinch to seal. Fasten with a toothpick.

6 Brush each wheel with a little milk and sprinkle with sesame or poppy seeds.

7 Bake according to directions on crescent roll package.

Serves 4

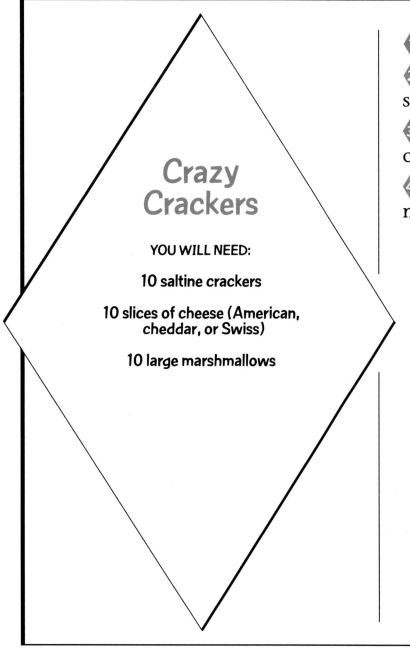

Crazy Crackers

YOU WILL NEED:

10 saltine crackers

10 slices of cheese (American, cheddar, or Swiss)

10 large marshmallows

1 Preheat oven to 350°.

2 Arrange crackers on a baking sheet.

3 Top each cracker with a slice of cheese and a marshmallow.

4 Bake crackers for about 5 minutes or until cheese is melted.

Makes 10

Strawberry Surprise Punch

YOU WILL NEED:

6 cups orange-pineapple juice, chilled

4 cups lemon-lime soda, chilled

orange slices

lemon slices

strawberry slices

1️⃣ In a punch bowl or a large pitcher, combine orange-pineapple juice and lemon-lime soda and stir.

2️⃣ Add orange, lemon, and strawberry slices.

Serves 10 to 15

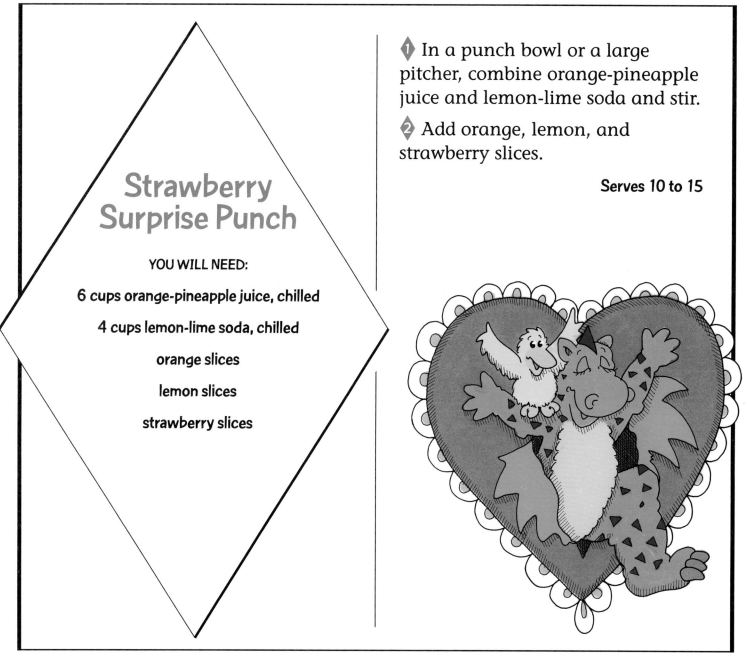

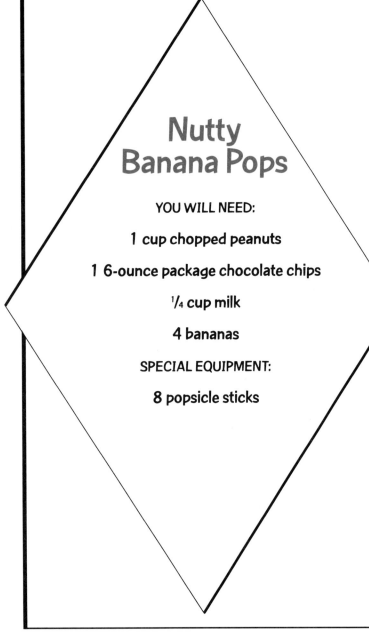

Nutty Banana Pops

YOU WILL NEED:

1 cup chopped peanuts

1 6-ounce package chocolate chips

$\frac{1}{4}$ cup milk

4 bananas

SPECIAL EQUIPMENT:

8 popsicle sticks

1. Pour nuts onto a plate.

2. Line a baking sheet with waxed paper.

3. Combine chocolate chips and milk in a medium saucepan. Cook over medium-low heat, stirring constantly, until chocolate is melted. To microwave, combine chocolate chips and milk in a microwave-safe dish. Microwave on high for 1 minute. Stir well. Continue to microwave on high for 20 seconds at a time, stirring after each heating, until chocolate is melted.

4. Peel bananas. Cut each banana in half the short way. Insert a popsicle stick into the flat, cut side of each banana.

5 Pick up a banana by the popsicle stick. Dip banana in melted chocolate then roll in peanuts. Set banana on cookie sheet. Repeat with remaining bananas.

6 Freeze bananas for at least 1 hour before serving.

Serves 8

Be a Valentine Detective

BLF XIZXPVW GSV XLWV!

Are you having trouble reading that sentence? That's because it's in code! This simple code will help you keep your valentine messages private. (But don't forget to tell your valentine how to read the code.) To begin with, write out the alphabet, like this:

A B C D E F G H I J K L M N O P Q R S T U V W X Y Z

Then write it out again underneath the first alphabet, but this time write it backwards, like this:

A B C D E F G H I J K L M N O P Q R S T U V W X Y Z
Z Y X W V U T S R Q P O N M L K J I H G F E D C B A

To write in code, simply substitute the bottom letter for the top letter. For instance, if you wanted to say "hello," you would write "svool." To read a coded message, just substitute the top letter for the bottom letter. Now that you know the secret, be a valentine detective and decode the message above.

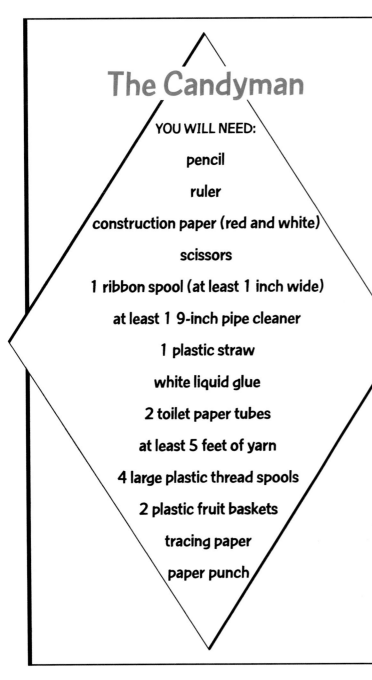

The Candyman

YOU WILL NEED:

pencil

ruler

construction paper (red and white)

scissors

1 ribbon spool (at least 1 inch wide)

at least 1 9-inch pipe cleaner

1 plastic straw

white liquid glue

2 toilet paper tubes

at least 5 feet of yarn

4 large plastic thread spools

2 plastic fruit baskets

tracing paper

paper punch

LOWER BODY:

❶ Draw two 4½- by 5¾-inch rectangles on red construction paper and cut them out.

❷ Apply a thin layer of white liquid glue to one of the rectangles and wrap it around a toilet paper tube. The ends will overlap slightly. Repeat with the other toilet paper tube.

❸ Measure ¼ inch down from the top of one of the toilet paper tubes and make an X. Measure ¼ inch down from top of the opposite side of the same toilet paper tube and make an X. Use a paper punch to punch a hole in each of the X's. Repeat with the other toilet paper tube.

❹ Cut four 4-inch pieces of yarn. Place the fruit basket upside down in front of you. Tie the toilet paper legs to the bottom of the basket with the yarn, using the holes you punched in step 3. (Use one piece of yarn for each hole.) The legs should be positioned so that a corner of the basket is facing forward. Trim the ends of the yarn.

5 Measure ¾ inch from the bottom of the front of the left leg. Make an X. Measure ¾ inch to the left of the first X and make a second X. Measure ¾ inch from the bottom of the front of the right leg. Make an X. Measure ¾ inch to the right of the first X and make a second X. Use a paper punch to punch a hole in each of the X's.

6 Remove the paper from the ends of a thread spool. Cut a 6-inch piece of yarn. Thread the yarn through one of the holes inside the spool and bring it back through one of the other holes. Tie the spool to one of the legs, using the holes you punched in step 5. Trim the ends of the yarn. Repeat with a second spool.

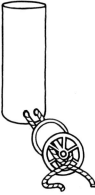

7 Place tracing paper on top of figure C on page 31 and trace. Cut out tracing paper pattern. Place the pattern on construction paper and trace around it. Move the pattern and trace around it again. Cut out two construction paper hearts.

8 Glue construction paper hearts to the ends of the spools to make the feet.

UPPER BODY:

1 Cut two 15-inch pieces of yarn. Place the second fruit basket upside down in front of you. Loop the yarn around the ribbon spool (the head) and tie it to the bottom of the basket. The head should be positioned so that a corner of the basket is facing forward.

2 Loop the second piece of yarn around spool and tie it to basket. Push one piece of yarn to one side of the spool and the other piece to the other side.

3 Thread pipe cleaner through the straw. Slide the straw through the sides of the second fruit basket so that it extends from one corner to another along the same line as the head.

4 Slide a spool on the end of the straw. Bend the pipe cleaner upward to secure the spool. Repeat with a second spool on the other end of the straw.

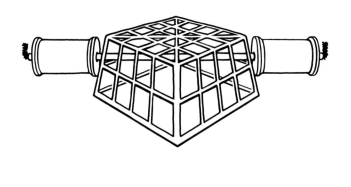

TO ASSEMBLE:

Place the open ends of the fruit baskets together. Along one side of the stacked baskets, tie two corners together with yarn. Allow the other corners to remain free so the basket can be opened and closed.

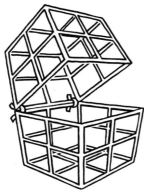

TO DECORATE:

Decorate the Candyman with yarn, pipe cleaners, and construction paper shapes attached with white liquid glue. You can use figure C to make more hearts to attach to the Candyman.

Don't forget to fill the Candyman's basket with candy!

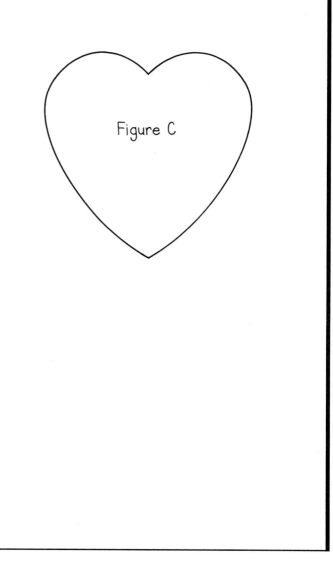

Figure C

Think Pink!

Super Simple Lasagne
▼
In the Pink Applesauce
▼
Cherry Cheese Tarts
▼
Three-D Valentine

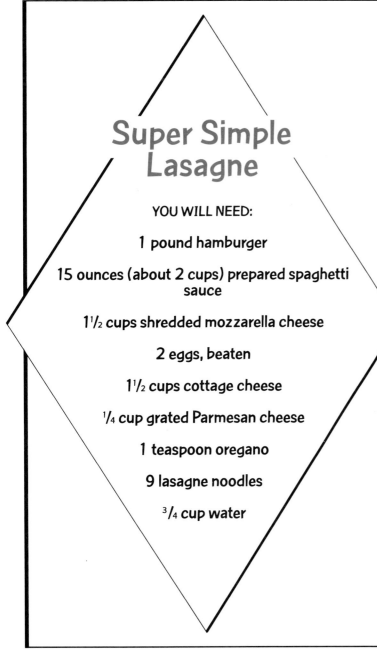

Super Simple Lasagne

YOU WILL NEED:

1 pound hamburger

15 ounces (about 2 cups) prepared spaghetti sauce

1½ cups shredded mozzarella cheese

2 eggs, beaten

1½ cups cottage cheese

¼ cup grated Parmesan cheese

1 teaspoon oregano

9 lasagne noodles

³/₄ cup water

1 Preheat oven to 350°.

2 Brown the hamburger in a large skillet. Remove from stove and drain off the grease.

3 Add spaghetti sauce to the hamburger and stir well.

4 In a small bowl, combine 1 cup mozzarella cheese (set aside the other ½ cup of mozzarella), eggs, cottage cheese, Parmesan cheese, and oregano. Stir well.

5 Grease a 9- by 13-inch baking pan.

6 Place three uncooked noodles on the bottom of the pan. Top with a third of the meat mixture and a third of the cheese mixture. Layer noodles, meat, and cheese two more times.

7 Pour the water around the edges of the pan.

◈ Cover with foil and bake 1 hour and 15 minutes. Uncover and sprinkle with remaining ½ cup of cheese. Bake for 5 minutes longer or until cheese is melted.

◈ Let stand 10 minutes before cutting.

Serves 6

The First Valentine

No one knows exactly how Valentine's Day started. One of the many stories about the holiday's beginnings takes place in Rome in the year 270. It is said there was a Christian priest named Valentine who was put in jail for refusing to worship the Roman gods. Valentine was a good man, who had always been kind to children. When the children of Rome heard of Valentine's trouble, they came to his jail cell to let him know they were thinking of him. The children wrote little notes and passed them through the bars on Valentine's window. These notes were the first valentines. The priest was put to death on February 14, the day we now celebrate as Valentine's Day.

In the Pink Applesauce

YOU WILL NEED:

4 apples, cored, peeled, and quartered

1/3 cup water

1/4 cup sugar

1/4 cup honey

1 tablespoon cinnamon candies

1 In a large saucepan, combine apples and water. Cook over medium heat for 20 to 30 minutes, stirring occasionally, until apples are soft.

2 Mash apples with the back of a spoon.

3 Add sugar, honey, and cinnamon candies and stir until candies are dissolved.

4 Reduce heat to medium-low and cook for 15 more minutes, stirring often.

Serves 4 to 6

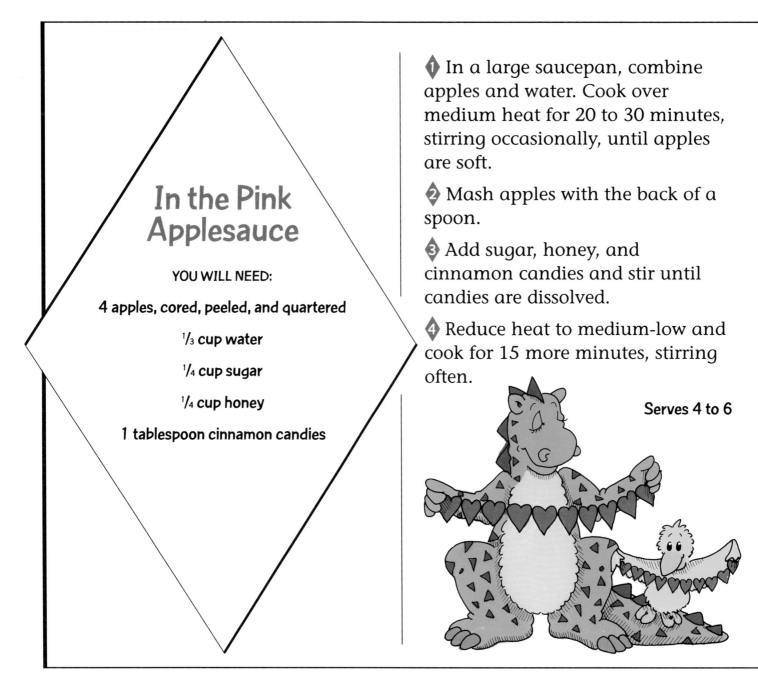

Cherry Cheese Tarts

YOU WILL NEED:

15 vanilla wafer cookies

3 3-ounce packages cream cheese

$\frac{1}{3}$ cup sugar

1 teaspoon orange juice

$\frac{1}{2}$ teaspoon almond extract

1 egg

1 12-ounce can cherry pie filling

SPECIAL EQUIPMENT:

12 paper muffin liners

1 Preheat oven to 375°.

2 Place cookies in a plastic bag and close tightly with a bread tie. Crush with a rolling pin.

3 Place 12 paper liners in a muffin tin.

4 Divide cookie crumbs evenly among muffin cups.

5 Combine cream cheese, sugar, orange juice, almond extract, and egg in a medium bowl. With an electric mixer, beat mixture for about 5 minutes, or until fluffy, on medium speed.

6 Divide cream cheese mixture evenly among muffin cups.

7 Bake for 20 to 25 minutes or until the tops of tarts are firm.

8 Cool 1 hour, then top each tart with pie filling.

Makes 12

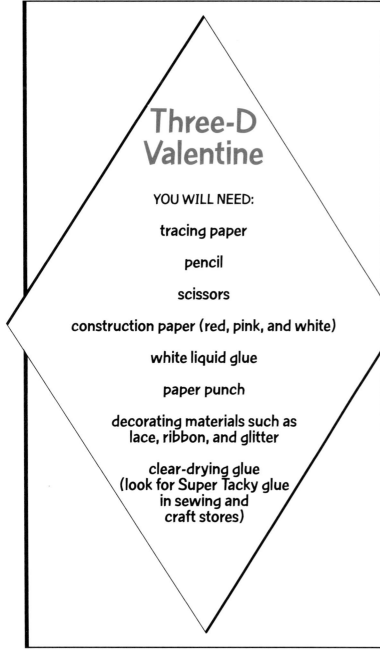

Three-D Valentine

YOU WILL NEED:

tracing paper

pencil

scissors

construction paper (red, pink, and white)

white liquid glue

paper punch

decorating materials such as
lace, ribbon, and glitter

clear-drying glue
(look for Super Tacky glue
in sewing and
craft stores)

1 Place tracing paper on top of figure B on page 19 and trace. Cut out tracing paper pattern.

2 Place the pattern on construction paper and trace around it. Move pattern and trace around it again. Repeat three more times to make five hearts in all. Cut out construction paper hearts.

3 Set one heart aside. Fold each of the remaining hearts in half lengthwise. Using a pencil, number the folded hearts 1 through 4. (These numbers won't show once valentine is assembled.)

4 Label hearts 1 through 4 with a side A and B as shown.

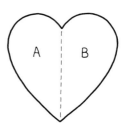

5 Use white liquid glue to glue side B of heart 1 to side A of heart 2. Glue side B of heart 2 to side A of heart 3. Glue side B of heart 3 to side A of heart 4.

6 Glue side B of heart 4 and side A of heart 1 to the heart that was set aside in step 3.

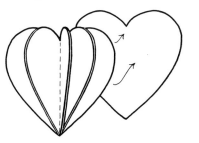

7 Use a paper punch to punch a hole in each side of the valentine as shown.

8 Use your imagination to decorate your valentine. Attach ribbon and lace with clear-drying glue. Use white liquid glue to attach construction paper shapes.

9 Use the holes in the valentine to attach it to a hairpin or a shoelace.

Cross My Heart

"Heart-y" Seafood Pies

▼

Cupid's Pepperoni Bread

▼

Not Just a Peanut Butter Sandwich

▼

Coconut Dreams

▼

Rainbow Smoothie

▼

Heartful Mobile

"Heart-y" Seafood Pies

YOU WILL NEED:

1 6½-ounce can tuna, drained

1 cup shredded American cheese

2 tablespoons sweet pickle relish

2 cans refrigerator biscuits
(10 biscuits per can)

flour

SPECIAL EQUIPMENT:

1 heart-shaped cookie cutter

1. Preheat oven to 375°.

2. In a small bowl, combine tuna, cheese, and pickle relish. Stir well.

3. Place a biscuit on a piece of waxed paper. Flatten the biscuit with the palm of your hand until it is about 5 inches in diameter. Repeat with 11 more biscuits.

4. Arrange six of the flattened biscuits on a baking sheet. Place a heaping tablespoon of the tuna mixture in the center of each biscuit.

5. Place the remaining six flattened biscuits on top of the tuna mixture. Press the tines of a fork around each pie to seal the edges.

6. Roll the remaining eight biscuits into a single ball. With a floured rolling pin, roll the dough out on a flat, floured surface until dough is about ¼-inch thick.

7 Cut six hearts out of the dough with cookie cutter. Place one heart on top of each pie. Gently press edges of hearts into pies to secure.

8 If you like, you can add other decorations to the pies with the remaining dough.

9 Bake for 12 to 15 minutes or until golden brown.

Serves 6

The Language of Flowers

During the 1800s, people often sent a valentine message in a special language: the language of flowers. Each plant had a meaning, and a bouquet of flowers could be "read" just like a valentine card.

Here are some flowers and their meanings to help you put together a message of your own.

Rose: Love

Ivy: Friendship

White chrysanthemum: Truth

Four-leafed clover: Be mine

Pansy: Thoughts

White clover: Think of me

Fool's parsley: Silliness

Marigold: Jealousy

Olive: Peace

White daisy: Innocence

Cupid's Pepperoni Bread

YOU WILL NEED:

1 loaf frozen bread dough

flour

4 ounces sliced pepperoni

1 cup shredded Swiss cheese

1 teaspoon Italian seasoning

1. Let the bread rise in the package in the refrigerator overnight.

2. Preheat oven to 350°.

3. Sprinkle a flat surface with flour. With a floured rolling pin, roll out dough into a 6- by 12-inch rectangle.

4. Arrange pepperoni slices in an even layer on bread dough.

5. Sprinkle cheese over pepperoni. Sprinkle lightly with Italian seasoning.

6. Roll up dough to make a long, narrow loaf and place seam side down on a baking sheet. Pinch ends of loaf together to seal in cheese.

7. Bake for 30 minutes or until golden brown.

8. Cool for at least 10 minutes before slicing.

Serves 6

Not Just a Peanut Butter Sandwich

YOU WILL NEED:

$3/4$ **cup peanut butter**

1 **cup chopped apple**

$1/2$ **cup shredded cheddar cheese**

8 **slices bread**

SPECIAL EQUIPMENT:

1 **heart-shaped cookie cutter (optional)**

1 In a small bowl, combine peanut butter, apple, and cheese.

2 Spread peanut butter mixture on four slices of bread. Top with remaining slices.

Serves 4

You can use a cookie cutter to cut bread into heart shapes if you like.

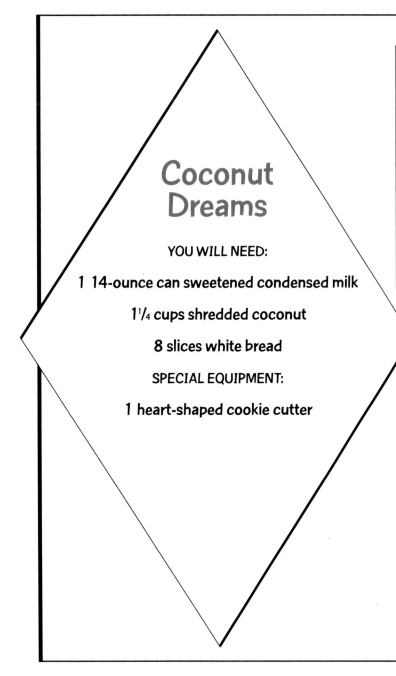

Coconut Dreams

YOU WILL NEED:

1 14-ounce can sweetened condensed milk

1¼ cups shredded coconut

8 slices white bread

SPECIAL EQUIPMENT:

1 heart-shaped cookie cutter

❶ Preheat oven to 350°.

❷ Pour milk into a shallow bowl. Place coconut in another shallow bowl.

❸ With cookie cutter, cut 2 hearts from each piece of bread to make 16 hearts.

❹ Dip one side of each heart in milk and then in coconut. Place hearts on baking sheet, coconut side up.

❺ Bake 6 to 7 minutes or until coconut begins to turn brown.

Makes 16

Rainbow Smoothie

YOU WILL NEED:

1 cup blueberries

1 cup blackberries

1 cup raspberries

2 small bananas, peeled

$\frac{1}{2}$ cup vanilla yogurt

4 ice cubes

2 sprigs fresh mint (optional)

1 Combine all ingredients except mint in a blender.

2 Blend for about 30 seconds or until smooth. Garnish with mint.

Serves 4

You can use either fresh or frozen fruit in this recipe.

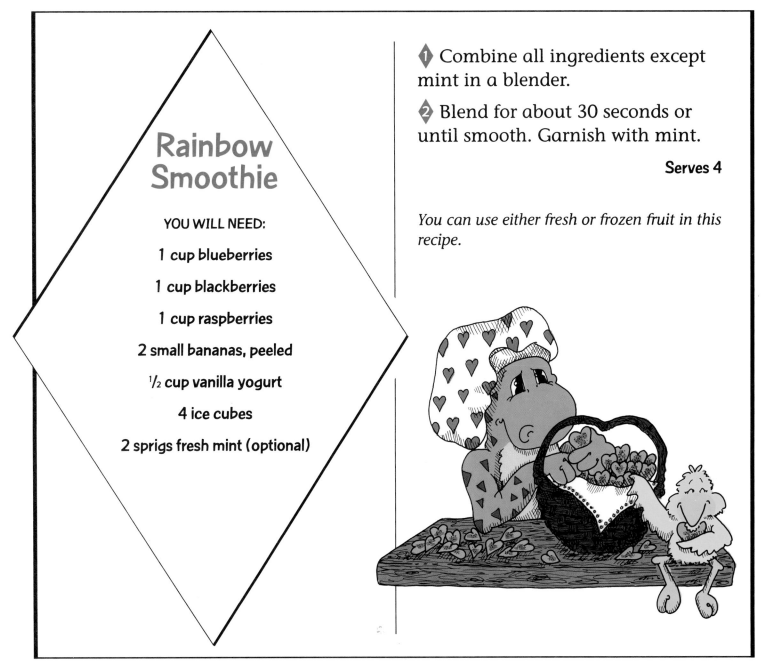

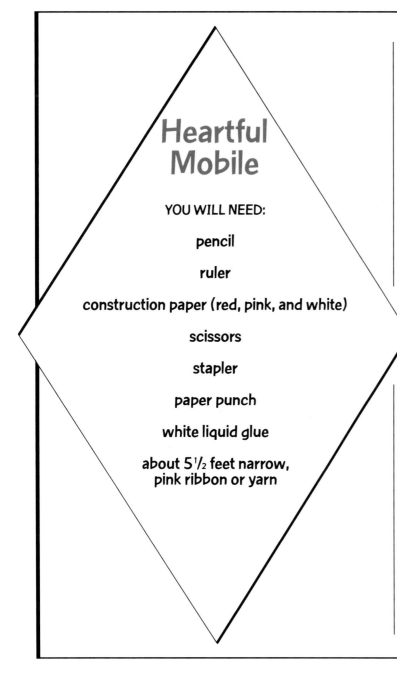

Heartful Mobile

YOU WILL NEED:

pencil

ruler

construction paper (red, pink, and white)

scissors

stapler

paper punch

white liquid glue

about 5½ feet narrow,
pink ribbon or yarn

❶ Draw two 10- by 1-inch strips on construction paper and cut them out. Draw two 8- by 1-inch strips on construction paper and cut them out. Draw two 6- by 1-inch strips on construction paper and cut them out.

❷ Place one of the 6-inch strips on top of the other, making sure to line the ends up evenly. Place an 8-inch strip on each side of the two 6-inch strips and line up the bottom edges. Place a 10-inch strip on each side of the two 8-inch strips and line up the bottom edges.

❸ Staple all of the strips together about ¼ inch from the bottom edges.

❹ Hold the strips of paper just above the staple. Take one of the 6-inch strips, loop it around on itself, and tuck the end in next to the staple. Repeat with the other 6-inch strip.

5 Loop an 8-inch strip around the 6-inch strip and tuck the end in next to the staple. Repeat with the second 8-inch strip and with both of the 10-inch strips.

6 Staple the ends of the strips in place about ¼ inch above the first staple.

staples

7 Repeat steps 1 through 6 four more times to make five hearts in all.

8 With a paper punch, punch two holes about ½ inch apart in the top of one of the hearts. Repeat with the remaining four hearts.

THE BASE:

1 Draw two 12- by 2-inch strips on construction paper and cut them out.

2 Glue the strips together so that the ends overlap by 1 inch. You will have formed a strip that is 23 inches long.

◆ Place the strip in front of you as shown. Draw a faint pencil line from one end of the strip to the other, ½ inch from the top of the strip.

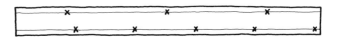

◆ Measure 4 inches from the end of the strip and make an X on the pencil line. Measure 7½ inches from the first X and make a second X on the pencil line. Measure 7½ inches from the second X and make a third X on the pencil line.

◆ Draw a faint pencil line from one end of the strip to the other, ½ inch from the bottom of the strip.

◆ Measure 4½ inches from the end of the strip and make an X on the pencil line. Measure 4½ inches from the first X and make a second

X. Repeat three more times to make five X's in all.

◆ Use a paper punch to punch a hole in each of the eight X's on the strip.

◆ Decorate the side of the strip without pencil lines with construction paper shapes attached with glue.

◆ Glue the ends of the strip together, overlapping the ends by 1 inch, to make a circle. Be sure the decorated side is facing out. Hold until glue has set. You will have covered up one of the holes. Repunch hole with paper punch.

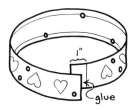

TO ASSEMBLE:

1 Cut five pieces of pink ribbon: one 12 inches long, one 10 inches long, one 8 inches long, one 6 inches long, and one 4 inches long.

2 Tie one end of one of the ribbons to one of the hearts you made earlier, using the holes punched in the tops of the hearts. Tie the other end of the ribbon to one of the five holes in the bottom of the base. Repeat with remaining hearts and ribbons.

3 Cut two 9-inch pieces of ribbon and one 16-inch piece of ribbon.

4 Tie one ribbon to each of the three holes at the top of the base.

5 Bring the three ribbons together about 6 inches from the top of the mobile and tie them together. There will be one piece that is much longer than the others. Use this piece to hang your mobile.

to be
YOUR
VALENTINE

me hanging
Valentine

Best Friends Lunch

Chicken for Chums

▼

Valentine Fruit Pizza

▼

Strawberries on a Stick

▼

Mousy Valentine

Chicken for Chums

YOU WILL NEED:

2 cups uncooked
long grain rice (not instant)

4 chicken breast halves

$1/8$ teaspoon salt

$1/8$ teaspoon pepper

3 cups milk

1 $10^3/4$-ounce can cream of chicken soup

1 $10^3/4$-ounce can
cream of celery soup

1 cup shredded
American cheese

1 Preheat oven to 350°.

2 Grease a 9- by 13-inch baking pan.

3 Place rice in greased baking pan.

4 Place chicken breasts, skin side up, on top of rice. Sprinkle with salt and pepper.

5 In a saucepan, combine milk, soups, and cheese. Cook over medium-low heat, stirring constantly, until cheese is melted.

6 Pour soup mixture over chicken.

7 Cover pan with foil and bake for 45 minutes or until chicken is tender and no longer pink in the center.

Serves 4

Fortune-Teller

Who likes you? Is your best friend mad at you? Will you receive a special valentine this year? Play Fortune-Teller and find out. You will need at least three people (the more people, the better), a blank sheet of paper, and a pencil. Arrange yourselves in a circle, and choose someone to go first. Have that person write a question that can be answered with yes, no, or maybe at the top of the sheet of paper. The player might ask, "Will I get a bike for my birthday?" or "Is John mad at me?" or "Does Sarah like me?" The player then folds the paper over to cover up what is written and passes the paper on to the next player. That player must answer the question that is written on the paper—without ever seeing the question. The answer can be a simple yes, no, or maybe. Or the player can give a more creative answer, such as, "Only if it rains on Tuesday" or "If you wish for it, it will come true." The player then folds the paper over to cover up the answer and writes his or her own question below. The player folds the paper over to hide the question and passes it on to the next player. The paper is passed all the way around the circle in this manner. Once the person who started the game has answered the last question, it is time to unfold the paper and learn the answers to your questions.

Valentine Fruit Pizza

YOU WILL NEED:

2 packages refrigerator crescent rolls (12 rolls total)

1 8-ounce package cream cheese, softened

$\frac{1}{2}$ cup sugar

1 teaspoon vanilla extract

1 tablespoon lemon juice

1 cup water

2 bananas, sliced

2 cups fresh strawberries, sliced

other fruits in season (optional)

1 Preheat oven to temperature called for on crescent roll package.

2 Separate dough into triangular sections. Arrange triangles of dough side by side in a circle on a round 14-inch pizza pan. Press the edges of the dough together with your fingers to make one large circle of dough.

3 Bake for time called for on package.

4 In a small bowl, combine cream cheese, sugar, and vanilla and stir well.

5 When crust has cooled to room temperature, spread cream cheese mixture evenly over it.

6 In a small bowl, combine lemon juice and water. Toss bananas in lemon juice mixture and drain on paper towel.

7 Arrange fruit attractively on cream cheese.

Serves 6 to 8

Strawberries on a Stick

YOU WILL NEED:

3 cups mashed strawberries

1 cup water

$^2/_3$ cup sugar

1 envelope unsweetened strawberry or cherry drink mix

SPECIAL EQUIPMENT:

10 medium paper cups

10 popsicle sticks

1 In a medium bowl, combine strawberries, water, sugar, and drink mix. Stir until drink mix is dissolved.

2 Pour mixture into paper cups.

3 Cover each cup tightly with a double layer of foil. Push a popsicle stick through the center of the foil on top of each cup. The foil will hold the stick straight until the liquid freezes.

4 Freeze 4 to 6 hours.

5 Remove the foil and pull treats out of cups to serve.

Makes 10

Mousy Valentine

YOU WILL NEED:

tracing paper

pencil

scissors

construction paper
(red, pink, black, and white)

white liquid glue

clear-drying glue (look for
Super Tacky glue in
sewing and craft stores)

1 8-inch black pipe cleaner

8 inches of
1/8-inch-wide
pink ribbon

ruler

THE BODY:

1 Place tracing paper on top of figure D on page 61 and trace. Cut out tracing paper pattern.

2 Place the pattern on red construction paper and trace around it. Move pattern and trace around it again. Repeat three more times to make five hearts in all. Cut out construction paper hearts.

3 Set one of the red hearts aside to use for the head. Fold each of the remaining four hearts in half lengthwise. Using a pencil, number the folded hearts 1 through 4.

4 Label hearts 1 through 4 with a side A and B as shown.

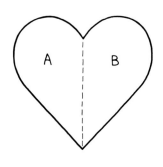

5 With white liquid glue, glue side B of heart 1 to side A of heart 2. Glue side B of heart 2 to side A of heart 3. Glue side B of heart 3 to side A of heart 4. Glue side B of heart 4 to side A of heart 1.

6 To attach the tail, apply clear-drying glue to one end of the pipe cleaner. Slide the pipe cleaner into the center of the body, where all four hearts come together. Allow to dry. Tie the pink ribbon around the end of the tail.

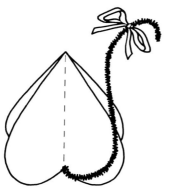

7 Place tracing paper on top of figure E on page 61 and trace. Cut out tracing paper pattern.

8 Place the pattern on pink construction paper and trace around it. Cut out construction paper heart.

9 Fold pink heart in half lengthwise. Use white liquid glue to glue the heart to the front of the mouse's body.

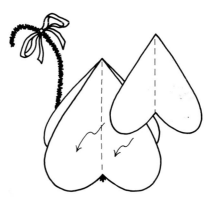

THE HEAD:

1 Place tracing paper on top of figure F on page 61 and trace. Cut out tracing paper pattern.

2 Place the pattern on pink construction paper and trace around it. Move the pattern and trace around it again. Cut out construction paper circles.

3 Place the heart you set aside earlier in front of you with the point facing down. Use white liquid glue to glue the pink circles to the top of the heart to make the ears.

4 Make your mouse some eyes, a nose, and some whiskers with black and white construction paper. Attach them with white liquid glue.

TO ASSEMBLE:

1 Place the body so that the pink-and-red heart is facing you, point side up. Measure 1¼ inches down from the point, along the side of the pink-and-red heart, and make a dot. Repeat on the other side of the same heart.

2 Use a scissors to cut a ¼-inch diagonal slit at each dot as shown. Slide the head into the two slits.

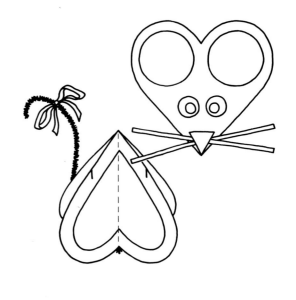

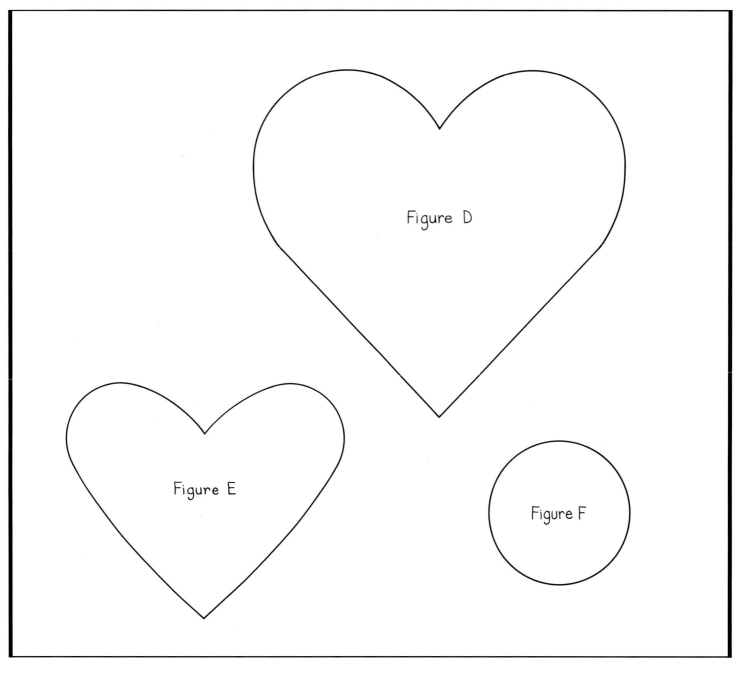

Figure D

Figure E

Figure F

Recipe List

Beverages

Strawberry Surprise Punch
Rainbow Smoothie

Side Dishes

Perfect Potato Casserole
Crazy Crackers
In the Pink Applesauce
Valentine Fruit Pizza

Main Dishes

Pork Chops Parmesan
Dizzy Ham Wheels
Super Simple Lasagne
"Heart-y" Seafood Pies
Cupid's Pepperoni Bread
Not Just a Peanut Butter Sandwich
Chicken for Chums

Desserts

Very-Berry Freeze Pie
Nutty Banana Pops
Cherry Cheese Tarts
Coconut Dreams
Strawberries on a Stick

Glossary

almond extract—a liquid used to give an almond flavor to food

beat—stir rapidly

brown—cook food, such as hamburger, until it is light brown

chill—refrigerate until cold

garnish—decorate with small pieces of food

grease—coat with a thin layer of butter, margarine, or shortening

Italian seasoning—a mixture of dried herbs, including basil and oregano

oregano—a fragrant herb often used in Italian food

paper punch—a device used to punch small, round holes in paper

perforated—having close-spaced holes for easy tearing

pipe cleaner—a wire enclosed in fuzzy fabric

poppy seeds—tiny, black seeds often sprinkled on breads and rolls

preheat—allow an oven to heat up to a certain temperature

rise—increase in size. This happens when the yeast in a dough produces carbon dioxide.

rolling pin—a cylinder with handles, used to roll out dough

sequin—a small, round, shiny piece of metal or plastic with a hole in the center

sesame seeds—small, oval seeds often sprinkled on breads and rolls

spool—a device used to hold materials such as ribbon, yarn, or thread

sweetened condensed milk—milk with some of the water removed and sugar added

sweet pickle relish—chopped up sweet pickles

thread—guide a material such as yarn or thread through a narrow opening, such as the eye of a needle

trace—copy a pattern onto another piece of paper

tracing paper—paper thin enough to be seen through when placed on top of a pattern

vanilla extract—a liquid used to give a vanilla flavor to food

waxed paper—wax-coated paper that is often used in baking because food won't stick to it

Worcestershire sauce—a strong-flavored, dark-brown liquid used to flavor food

Index